KETO DIET FOR

BEGINNERS

2021

The Ultimate Guide to the Ketogenic Diet for Beginners A 21-Day Food Plan to Lose Weight, Boost Metabolism and Stay Healthy, Including Simple and Delicious Recipes

Table of Contents

Introduction

Beginning a new lifestyle can be daunting. It doesn't matter if you know that the lifestyle promises many benefits such as weight loss and improved health without the drawbacks of crash or fad diets. Either way, a lifestyle change will impact your life, and you can be unsure of how to approach the change. But there is no need to fear. In this book, you will learn all you need to know about the ketogenic diet, how to transition onto it fully within thirty days, managing any side effects, pairing it with helpful exercises and supplements, many delicious recipes, and much more to get you well on your way toward success.

Why settle for a life where you are unhappily clinging to an idea of "someday" being at your ideal weight and health? Instead, with the knowledge in this book, you can reach out and grasp your dream, turning it into reality. You can live at a healthy weight full of vibrant energy, improved brain health, better sleep, and mouth-watering tasty meals. Losing weight and gaining health doesn't mean you have to deprive yourself of the best things in life.

To the people who have lived one crash diet to the next, this may sound like an impossible ideal. But I promise you it is not. You don't have to take my word for it, though. There is a century's worth of scientific studies proving the beneficial and sustainable effects of the ketogenic diet.

Not only can you gain an improved life on the ketogenic diet, but you can do it at your own pace. There is no need to throw yourself into something new while still unprepared. Rather, you won't just gain all the knowledge and tools you need within this book; you will also gain a plan to help you slowly transition onto a keto lifestyle in thirty days.

Reduce the Symptoms Experienced During the Keto Flu

The keto flu, while partially caused by detoxing from sugar, it's mostly caused by deficiencies developed the first couple weeks of ketosis. This is largely due to losing so much water weight that you also lose vital nutrients such as electrolytes. But, by replenishing these deficiencies, you can feel much better, increase energy, and fuel your body. But, there are also other supplements people use during the early phases of ketosis in order to help the entire process go more smoothly, quickly, and easily.

Get Any of the Nutrients You May Be Missing

It is certainly possible to get all of the nutrients you require on the ketogenic diet. But, because it is a new way of eating that greatly limits fruits and doesn't allow grains or starchy vegetables, some people may have trouble at first eating all of the nutrients they require. This will become easier over time as they adapt and learn to incorporate more whole keto foods into their daily lives. But, in the meantime, by taking vitamins and supplements, a person can prevent deficiencies while they adjust.

Work Toward Better Health

There are many health-promoting foods on the ketogenic diet, but sometimes we may want to target specific health goals. For instance, if you want to increase your brain health, you may specifically want to increase the amount of fish oil and MCT oil within your diet. You can certainly do this naturally by eating more fish and coconut oil, but you may also decide to supplement with a fish oil tablet.

There are many health-promoting foods, but it often easy to get all of them within our diet. Therefore, supplements can help us target specific health goals or overall health so that we can age better and decrease our risk of developing a disease.

Now that you understand why supplements can help with the ketogenic diet, let's have a look at which ones people often find the most benefit from.

#1: Exogenous Ketones

You already know that your body naturally produces ketones, but did you know that you can get them within a supplement, as well? Exogenous ketones have the same molecular structure as those found within your body. But, they can be bought in the form of a pill, powder, or liquid. Better yet, these are not some snake oil being peddled off. Studies have shown that these truly are effective and help put the body into a state of ketosis. In fact, scientific studies will sometimes use exogenous ketones solely to study how ketosis affects different aspects of health, such as our brain health.

There are multiple ways in which exogenous ketones can help, which includes:

- The keto flu, while partially caused by electrolyte deficiencies and dehydration, is also caused by sugar withdrawal. But, once your body is able to begin to create ketones, your body will adjust and feel an increase in energy. By taking exogenous ketones, you can speed this process up and either completely avoid the keto flu or speed it up quickly.

- If you find that you ate too many net carbohydrates, then taking exogenous ketones can help you maintain a state of ketosis. While eating a large number of carbs will usually kick a person out of ketosis, exogenous ketones are able to immediately increase your ketone levels, lower blood glucose levels, and manage the insulin response.

- A lot of people are looking to manage their appetite when losing weight. Ketones naturally do this by increasing your body's natural energy supply (ketones) and therefore suppressing your hunger. This is not an unhealthy way of suppressing hunger because the ketones are simply providing your body with the fuel it requires. In one study, it was found that after fasting overnight, if you take exogenous ketones, you can suppress your hunger by an additional four hours.

- Ketones naturally increase our cognitive and mental functioning, which is why the ketogenic diet is known to have such a potent effect on neurological and neurodegenerative diseases. Thankfully, one study has shown that by taking exogenous ketones, we can compound this effect. In one study, it was shown that by taking exogenous ketone supplements, participants were able to reduce anxiety.

When taking exogenous ketones, it is important that you follow the directions and only take the daily recommended amount. This is easy to find, as it should be on the label of all exogenous ketone products. If you are hoping to use exogenous ketones to decrease or prevent the keto flu, then begin to take them the same day that you start the ketogenic diet and proceed to take them for the following seven days. For people who hope to boost their energy and mental functioning, try taking ketones with your breakfast in the morning. And lastly, if you hope to boost your workout routine, you can take exogenous ketones directly before you exercise.

#2: MCT Oil

MCT, or medium-chain triglycerides, are a clear and tasteless oil or powder. While coconut oil has a high percentage of MCTs within it, if you want as many benefits from MCTs as possible when you choose to use pure MCT oil. The benefit of this type of fat is that not only can your body utilize it for fuel more quickly and easily than other fats, it also increases your ketone production. This can increase brain function, energy levels, weight loss, appetite management, and more.

We are able to benefit this way because our body naturally prefers to use ketones and MCTs for energy, rather than storing fuel as body day. Plus, MCTs are more quickly and easily digested by our bodies. Instead of having to go into the small intestines to be further digested, they are able to go directly to our liver to be used as fuel and transformed into ketones.

Studies have shown that MCTs are able to regulate our genes, which control the stored fat as well as our hormone receptors that impact our body's metabolism. This naturally leads to them being a powerful weight loss tool. Other studies have also shown that they can improve our body's natural insulin response, cholesterol, and blood glucose levels.

Since MCTs are flavorless and without a scent, you can easily add them to both savory and sweet dishes. You can even add MCTs to your coffee or tea! While you can take these at any time of the day, it is best to take them in the afternoon and morning. In the evening, they could increase your energy too much to allow you to sleep. Plus, you will most benefit from the increase in energy and fat burning during the daytime, as well.

#3: Collagen Peptides

Collagen is naturally present within our bodies. In fact, it is the most abundant type of protein, making up thirty percent of the total protein within our cells. This type of protein is critical for our tendons, skin, cartilage, bones, organs, and other connective tissues. While we are capable of creating collagen on our own, from eating various amino acids in food, we can also boost our collagen production with collagen peptides. These are a hydrolyzed type of collagen that is easily digested and utilized by the body. Some of the benefits of taking collagen peptides include healthier joints, stronger bones, increased skin health, decreased levels of inflammation, stronger muscles, and increased recovery from workouts.

Not only will you receive these benefits from collagen peptides, but there are some benefits unique to the ketogenic diet, as well. Since collagen is a type of easily digested protein, you can ensure you are eating enough protein to prevent the gluconeogenesis process from relying on the amino acids within your muscles. Collagen is also incredibly satiating and satisfying, helping to keep you energized and full while losing weight.

When choosing a brand of collagen peptides, it's important that you find a brand that is clean and reliable. You want one that doesn't contain artificial ingredients, fillers, or sugar. Ideally, the collagen should be sourced from grass-fed cows, pigs, or fish.

Using collagen peptides is incredibly easy. You simply use them as you would any other protein supplement. They can be added to shakes, coffee, tea, muffins, and more. In fact, you can just add it to water even! The taste is incredibly mild, meaning it shouldn't alter the flavor of whatever you are having it in by much, if at all. Enjoy taking collagen peptides whenever you need a boost in protein. You can especially benefit from the prior to a workout, during a mid-afternoon lull, or with your morning Ketorific coffee. Although, as always, be sure to follow the directions on the package and do not consume more than the recommended amount.

#4: Omega-3 Fish Oil Supplements

The best source of vital omega-3 fats is fish oil. Yet, most people often don't eat enough fish within their diets. Researchers surmise that this is one of the reasons that chronic illness and disease are on the rise in America and other Western countries. We need these fats in order to produce energy, allow our cells and molecules to communicate, produce cell membranes, lower inflammation, protect the brain, and more. To ensure you are getting enough of these amazing fatty acids, you can easily take a fish oil supplement. Although, you can also get omega-3s from fortified eggs, walnuts, broccoli, avocados, chia seeds, and flaxseeds.

Along with protecting your health, the fatty acids within omega-3s will help to balance your omega-3 to the omega-6 ratio, which is essential for our body's natural inflammation response. Along with this, the fats can help us to maintain a healthy high-fat diet and ketosis.

#5: Electrolytes

As we have mentioned, during the beginning stages of ketosis, your body will naturally lose a lot of water as well as electrolytes through urination while your blood glucose level decreases. This is a normal part of ketosis, but you need to ensure that you are replenishing what your body is losing. Not only do you need to drink more water than usual, but you need to focus on either naturally consuming electrolytes or supplementing with them. By doing this, not only will you be able to manage the keto flu symptoms, but you will also be able to maintain your health. There are four electrolytes that you need to focus on consuming. These are sodium, magnesium, potassium, and calcium.

Sodium is often talked about negatively because many Americans consume too much in their high junk food diet. But, when you switch to keto, not only will you lose a lot of sodium through the ketosis process, but you also won't be consuming nearly as much. To top that off, the ketogenic diet is known to heal the insulin response, helping your body to not hold onto the excessive amount of sodium. Yet, just as excessive amounts of sodium can be detrimental, so too can a deficiency. This micronutrient is vital to support our nervous system and the amount of water within our cells. Without sodium, we can develop headaches, muscle spasms, fatigue, confusion, and heart palpitations.

Magnesium is the fourth most prominent mineral within our bodies. Because of this, it participates in over three-hundred biological functions such as our heart rate, muscle functioning, blood sugar, nerve health, and more. The most common symptoms of deficiency are muscle spasms, numbness, and fatigue.

Potassium pairs with sodium to help maintain a balance of water within our cells. It also plays a major role in controlling the natural electrical activity within our muscles and heart. Without potassium, we simply wouldn't be able to survive because our hearts would be unable to beat properly. While sodium is mostly found outside of our cells, potassium resides within them to help the cells and nerves communicate with one another. Deficiencies in potassium lead to constipation, fatigue, muscle weakness, and heartbeat irregularities.

Of all the minerals within our bodies, calcium is the most prevalent. Our bodies not only use it to strengthen our bones and teeth but also to aid in cell communication, nerve functioning, and the natural blood clotting process. If we experience a deficiency in this mineral, we can experience numbness, muscle spasms, and even seizures. Thankfully, these symptoms are rare because our body is able to take the calcium from our bones to stay stable. However, we don't want this because it can weaken the bones. Therefore, it is important to get calcium from plenty of sources.

Here is a chart of how many milligrams of the four main electrolytes that we require on a daily basis.

While you can supplement electrolytes, it's also important to incorporate them within your diet. Below is a list of electrolyte-rich foods sorted by each type of electrolyte.

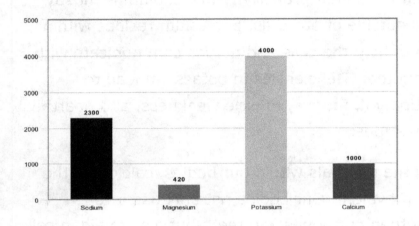

Sodium:	Magnesium:	Potassium:	Calcium:
• Ham	• Avocados	• Broccoli	• Broccoli
• Bacon	• Dark chocolate	• Bacon	• Kale
• Beef	• Nuts	• Salmon	• Bok Choy
• Sardines	• Flaxseeds	• Beef	• Chia seeds
		• Avocados	

• Dairy	• Tofu	• Mushrooms	• Sunflower seeds
• Eggs	• Chia seeds	• Cauliflower	
• Dark leafy greens	• Salmon	• Dark chocolate	• Sesame seeds
	• Dark leafy greens		• Sardines
• Celery			• Almonds
• Artichokes			• Canned salmon

While these are all great low-carb sources of electrolytes, you may need to also supplement. This is especially true during the first few weeks of ketosis. It's ideal and superior to get these naturally within your diet, but a supplement is also superior to becoming deficient.

Two ways you can add these to your diet is by using drink mixes or pills. For drink mixes, there is a keto sports drink, Ultima Replenisher. There is also an exogenous ketone sports drink. This has the benefit of containing not only the electrolytes you need but electrolytes and other micronutrients, as well. The brand that produces this is Perfect Keto, and the drink is their Lemon Keto Perform.

If you want to go the pill route, you can easily take an electrolyte pill. These can be found in vitamin and mineral shops and online. These pills are convenient because they contain a large number of electrolytes in an easy to take form.

Chapter 6: Intermittent Fasting

When you first hear the term 'intermittent fasting' it may bring to mind unhealthy fad diets, crash diets, and cleanses. But, unlike these unhealthy fads that promote nutrient deficiencies and decreased health, intermittent fasting is only done for short periods of time and promotes health and healing. In fact, many studies have been conducted that not only prove that intermittent fasting is effective for weight loss but for improved health, as well.

While you don't have to practice intermittent fasting on the ketogenic diet, the two work together beautifully. This is because intermittent fasting is processed by the body nearly identically as the ketogenic diet since both activate ketosis. This means that intermittent fasting is much easier to practice when you are already in a state of ketosis than when someone is not. It will feel easier and natural during ketosis.

When you are on either the ketogenic diet or intermittent fasting, your body will begin to use up all of the stored glycogen that is within your liver and muscles. You should run out of glucose between six and twenty-four hours if you are not diabetic. Afterward, your body will begin to convert the amino acids from the protein you have eaten into glucose for the few select cells that require this nutrient. Soon after that begins, your body will begin to convert fats into ketones for fuel. These have many benefits, especially when it is from the ketogenic diet and intermittent fasting paired together.

To fully understand why you should consider intermittent fasting, you first need to know of its many benefits. Whether you are healthy or ill, average weight or overweight, you can gain benefits from including this process within your lifestyle.

Improved Weight Loss

Usually, our bodies are constantly focusing on digesting the meals we have eaten, using them as fuel, or storing them for use later on. This means that our level of body fat gradually increases. But, when you are fasting, you give your body a chance to use the very fat that is stored for use. You will find that you naturally lose weight, but because the fasts are short, you are able to do so without hunger or nutrient deficiencies.

One study conducted in 2014 found that when participants fasted over a period of three to four weeks, they were able to greatly decrease their body weight. In fact, the participants lost between 3 to 8% of their weight.

An Increase in Important Hormones

While most people never consider the state of their hormones, they are incredibly important. The human growth hormone, which is produced in our pituitary gland, is one of these vital hormones. Some of its jobs include maintaining tissue health, increasing muscle mass, protecting bone density, maintaining brain health, growing and regenerating cells, and more.

When we are fasting, this amazing hormone greatly increases. In fact, it can raise up to five times its average level! This is wonderful because it can help us lose less muscle as we age, lowers fat tissue, protects cardiovascular health, maintains bone health, and maintains skin health and thickness.

Transmutes Fat

Along with helping us to lose weight, animal studies suggest that fasting can help us to convert our unhealthy white fat into a better type of fat. While most people simply think that fat is fat, there are actually multiple types. These different types of fat have various effects on our health, some positive, and some detrimental. White fat is the most common and unhealthy. But, brown fat is much better for our body and even helps our metabolism to better burn off our white fat. When fasting, your body will begin to transmute the unhealthy white fat into brown fat, thereby promoting your health and weight loss.

Increases Metabolism

Going from one diet to the next, greatly restricting calories, and refraining from eating for long periods are greatly damaging to the metabolism. You will also find that your metabolism naturally slows down as you age, which is why a lot of fifty-year-olds no longer look like they did in their twenties. But, studies have shown that if you practice intermittent fasting regularly and then consume a meal afterward, you can increase your metabolism, burn more fat, and retain your lean muscle mass.

Boost Energy

Just as the ketogenic diet increases the production of the all-important mitochondrial cells, so too does intermittent fasting. By increasing these cells, you can better convert food into fuel and then carry it to the cells that require it for energy. Not only that but even more cells, such as those in your brain, will be able to process ketones for fuel rather than glucose. Since these cells provide ninety percent of the energy our bodies require, w can greatly boost both our physical and mental well-being by increasing our mitochondrial cells.

Prevent Muscle Loss

Many people begin to lose their lean muscle mass when they diet. This is bad because we require this muscle mass for our health. If we lose too much, it can even affect our hearts. Thankfully, a study conducted in 2011, showed that we are able to lose fat with intermittent fasting, but unlike people who diet we won't lose as much muscle.

Treat Insulin Resistance

Insulin resistance increases our chance of diabetes, prevents our body from properly transporting glucose, increases blood sugar spikes and crashes, and adds to weight gain. But, studies have found that intermittent fasting is successful in treating this condition. Not only that, but it can also reduce high blood sugar.

Decrease Chronic Inflammation

While inflammation may be a normal and healthy part of our immune systems, it can become chronically high and worsen our health over time. Conditions such as cancer, arthritis, heart disease, or even a diet full of toxins can damage our inflammation response. Thankfully, studies have shown that by practicing intermittent fasting throughout the period of a month a person can greatly reduce their inflammation levels.

Slow Down Aging

Scientists are not sure of the reasons behind this, but they have found clear evidence that the practice of intermittent fasting not only decreases aging but even increases our lifespan. Scientists have found this to be true in multiple animal and human studies. Scientists hypothesize that one of the causes behind this may be the way in which fasting affects our mitochondrial cells.

Prevent Oxidative Stress

One of the other factors that greatly affect our aging, the chance of disease, and overall health is oxidative stress caused by free radicals. These damaging free radicals affect cells throughout our bodies, slowly causing them harm. As these cells become damaged, we are beginning to age more quickly and become more prone to disease. However, studies have found that intermittent fasting makes a large impact on the oxidative stress within our bodies and can greatly decrease the damage while increasing beneficial antioxidants.

Cares for the Heart

Heart disease is one of the leading causes of death, not just in America, but worldwide. Statistics show that conditions of the heart cause over thirty-one percent of the annual global deaths. Thankfully, we also know that we can greatly impact our heart health by changing our lifestyles. Both the ketogenic diet and intermittent fasting have been found to be two of the beneficial lifestyle changes that we can make. One study found that people who fasted every other day for eight weeks were able to reduce their bad cholesterol (LDL) by a major twenty-five percent! As if that weren't good enough, they also were able to reduce their blood triglycerides by thirty-two percent. In an additional study, obese adults were able to greatly reduce their blood triglycerides, bad cholesterol, total cholesterol, and blood pressure.

Reduce the Risk of Cancer

The studies on cancer and intermittent fasting are still in their early phases and need more work. Specifically, we require more studies on human participants to fully see how intermittent fasting affects cancer prevention and treatment. But, the preliminary studies have shown that fasting every other day can stop the growth of tumors in animals. Similarly, both animal and test-tube studies have found intermittent fasting an effective means of preventing cancer. One test-tube study even found that fasting was equally as effective as chemotherapy in stopping the growth of tumors. Finally, studies have also found that fasting combined with chemotherapy can increase the effectiveness of both forms of treatment.

Increase Brain Function

There is great evidence that suggests intermittent fasting may improve and protect brain health. This is especially beneficial with rates of Alzheimer's disease on the rise and other diseases such as Parkinson's disease and multiple sclerosis. In one primary study on mice, it was found that by intermittent fasting for eleven months they were greatly able to improve not only the function of their brain but its very structure. Another study found that fasting was able to improve cognitive functioning, increase the production of nerve cells, and improve overall brain health.

Manage Epilepsy and Prevent Seizures

Intermittent fasting, especially when paired with the ketogenic diet, is wonderful for epilepsy. After all, the ketogenic diet was first inspired by the effectiveness of fasting in treating epilepsy. There are many studies that prove the effectiveness of fasting for treating epilepsy, and when combined with the ketogenic diet it can especially help people who have difficulty controlling seizures.

Promote Cellular Repair

Our body has a normal and healthy process known as autophagy. This process is incredibly important as it helps to recycle our old and unhealthy cells that could compromise our health. Once the old cells are gone, they are then replaced with healthier cells that can promote our health. As you can see, autophagy is vital for our health and the prevention of disease. It is so important that scientists are attempting to create drugs that have the ability to cross the blood-brain barrier and trigger this response. But, they haven't been able to find a drug solution as of yet. However, there is a natural option that we can use in our daily lives to promote this process, which is intermittent fasting. Not only does intermittent fasting help trigger the process of autophagy, but it also helps the cells activate their self-regenerative state.

Promote the Growth of Brain Cells

Not only are neurological and neurodegenerative diseases becoming more prevalent, but many people suffer from mental illnesses such as anxiety, depression, and bipolar disorder. Yet, intermittent fasting may help. Studies have found that fasting is able to increase neurogenesis within the brain, which then increases the growth of brain cells and nerve tissues. Studies have shown that by increasing the process of neurogenesis, we can improve mood, focus, memory, and overall brain performance. This is thanks due to the brain-derived neurotrophic factor, commonly known as BDNF. By stimulating our BDNF, we can boost cell growth within our cortex, hippocampus, basal forebrain, and other areas of our nervous system.

As you can see, fasting has many benefits when done correctly. But, in order to incorporate it into your diet in a healthy and seamless fashion, you need to understand how our body responds differently in both the fasted and the fed state.

When we eat food, we enter the fed state, which lasts for three to five hours afterward while our body works on digesting the food and absorbing all of its nutrients. When we are in this state, our body is unlikely to burn any of our body fat because our body is attempting to burn off the fuel we have just eaten and our insulin levels are raised.

Once the fed state is over, we enter the post-absorptive state. This state is when people have finished digesting any and all food, they are more likely to burn body fat, and their insulin levels are low. This state commonly lasts between eight and twelve hours.

After the post-absorptive state comes to the fasted state, usually twelve hours after we have last eaten a meal. While this state is common, most people within Western societies never enter a fasted state. But, if you are able to reach this state you can lose weight must more easily and without much effort. Even without changing how much you are eating, what you eat, or your exercise routine you will be able to burn the stored fat within your body and lose weight.

Many people may feel that it's unhealthy and unnatural to fast. After all, is it any different from starvation? The answer is that yes, it is different! Fasting is intentional, meaning you are able to completely control your circumstances, what you eat, how much you eat, and how frequently you eat. When starving people typically are not consuming the nutrients or calories they require. Whereas with intermittent fasting you can be sure that prior to and after fasting you are able to eat everything your body requires. For instance, it's not unhealthy to skip breakfast as long as you eat all of your needed nutrients with your lunch and dinner.

Americans are used to eating frequently, more frequently than is healthy. Life requires balance for a healthy body, and by utilizing intermittent fasting, we can attain the balance that our bodies crave.

Lastly, before we teach you how to practice intermittent fasting, let's go over some frequently asked questions.

Don't I Need to Eat Frequently to Boost My Metabolism?

It's a common myth that we must eat smaller meals throughout the day rather than larger meals in order to boost our metabolism. Because this myth has been purported so frequently, it is now believed as truth, even without having a single piece of scientific truth behind it. This myth was started because of our metabolic rate. When we eat, this metabolic rate slightly raises for a few hours, but it also requires energy in order to digest and absorb the food we have eaten. The amount of energy we must expend in this process depends on how many calories and nutrients we have eaten. This is known as the thermic effect of food. Let's have a look at how a two-thousand calorie diet affects us when spread between different meal sizes.

If we were to eat six small meals, each would be approximately three-hundred and thirty-three calories. Three meals a day would be about six-hundred and sixty-six. Lastly, two meals would each be one-thousand calories.

When we eat these meals, you will find that your metabolism slightly increases due to the thermic effect of the foods. However, this effect alters depending on how many calories you have eaten. The first example with six separate meals only barely raises the metabolic rate. On the other hand, the last example can greatly boost the metabolic rate, which will slowly fade throughout the day.

However, while all three examples boost our metabolic rate, none of them is superior to another. The third example may have a larger effect, but it doesn't last as long. On the other hand, the first example only has a small boost, but it will last throughout most of the day as you are frequently eating. The truth is that whichever method you choose at the end of the day, your body will have taken the same amount of energy to process and absorb the nutrients you have eaten.

Each example may be different, but the benefit you receive is identical in each circumstance. Even if you want to use the thermic effect to your advantage, there is no way you can benefit from one of these instances over another. Your body simply is not going to be fooled into burning more calories.

What About Controlling Hunger?

More scientific research is needed on meal size and hunger, as there are surprisingly few studies that have been conducted. However, the research that has been done indicates that we can gain better control of our appetites by eating fewer large meals that are high in protein.

But, more important than the size and frequency of our meals is what we are eating. For instance, we know that glucose is processed by the body much more quickly than fat and protein. This leads to foods such as breakfast cereal and cake, leading people to be hungry quickly, even if they ate seven-hundred calories worth. But, if you eat seven-hundred calories of a nutrient-dense ketogenic meal full of healthy fats and proteins, then you will feel that you are naturally full and satisfied for long periods of time. Of course, this is more effective when you have already been in ketosis for a few weeks and are fully keto-adapted.

Isn't Breakfast the Most Important Meal of the Day?

We regularly hear that breakfast is the most important meal of the day, so why do people practicing intermittent fasting often skip breakfast? Firstly, while skipping breakfast may be associated with weight gain, that doesn't mean that it is caused by skipping breakfast. Instead, this weight gain is most often caused by eating in a reckless manner. People who skip breakfast often develop hunger later on in the day and end up overeating. Similarly, they might grab junk food while out, such as doughnuts or fast food. And lastly, some people skip breakfast while on crash diets. We know full well the danger of these diets and that they cause damage to the metabolism and are likely to cause long-term weight gain.

Statistics show that people who skip breakfast are less likely to eat balanced and nutritious meals later on in the day. This makes it obvious to see why those who skip breakfast are more likely to gain weight. It's not because breakfast is somehow magically more powerful and impactful than lunch or dinner.

What About the Starvation Mode?

We know full well that the metabolic rate is lower when the body is in starvation mode. This is to help humans during times of famine to survive as long as possible until they can find a new source of food. But, the fact is that starvation and fasting are not the same things. Starvation is long-term, whereas intermittent fasting usually only lasts for twelve or sixteen hours, but never more than twenty-four hours. Fasting for this period of time simply won't cause the body to enter the starvation mode.

In fact, studies indicate that the metabolic rate doesn't slow down until a person has been without food for a minimum of sixty hours. Other studies found that this slowing down didn't even begin until hour seventy-two to ninety-six of going without food.

On the other hand, intermittent fasting has been shown to frequently increase our metabolic rate. In some studies, short-term fasting has increased the metabolic rate by 3 to 10%.

Doesn't Fasting Cause Muscle Loss?

Food is important for not only growing muscles but maintaining muscles. This is especially true when you are in a state of ketosis, and your body is naturally converting amino acids into glucose for the brain cells. If you don't eat enough protein, then the gluconeogenesis process will resort to taking the amino acids from your muscles.

But, protein is absorbed into our bodies at a much slower rate than other fuel sources. The result is that if we eat a high protein meal such as a large burger patty, an avocado, cheese, mushrooms, tomato, and bacon, then we consume a large number of amino acids. These can slowly be absorbed into our bodies over the course of sixteen to twenty-four hours. The result is that with the slow process of digestion, you will likely stay fueled with protein the entire time you are fasting. Even if you decide to fast for twenty hours and your protein was fully absorbed after sixteen hours, it won't cause any harm to your body as long as you are eating your entire ratio of protein when you aren't fasting.

As long as you are not fasting for over twenty-four hours and are eating your full protein recommendation, then you will experience no muscle loss.

But I've Been Told You Can't Exercise on an Empty Stomach?

Remember, fasting on its own does not cause muscle loss when done correctly. But, you may still worry about if you can complete your workout routine while fasted. Thankfully, there have been many studies done on this.

There is a large body of evidence and research on fitness during Ramadan when Muslims fast during the day. These studies all concur that light to moderate exercises and aerobics are unaffected by fasting, even if the person has been fasting for three solid days. Not only that, but there was no loss in muscle tone, and fat burning was more effective when exercising while fasting.

As you can see, intermittent fasting is perfectly safe. Now that you have a full understanding of fasting, let's look at the different methods you can try.

Meal Skipping

One of the most natural ways to practice intermittent fasting is by meal skipping. This method is especially wonderful for beginners because it fits into your schedule, prevents hunger, requires no scheduling, and will keep you energized. This method of fasting is as simple as skipping a meal when you find you are not hungry. For instance, one day you may skip breakfast, or another, you may skip lunch. This method doesn't have as many health benefits as the longer fasting methods, but it is a great way to work your way into intermittent fasting and built up the length of time you feel comfortable going without eating.

This method is most successful when a person doesn't try to force it. Rather than making yourself skip a meal, wait until you aren't hungry and it feels natural. If you try to force it, you will only end up overeating later and undoing any benefits you might have gained. Let it stay organic, not forced.

12/12

By far, the easiest method of scheduled fasting is the 12/12 method. This method is simple, during twelve hours of the day, you refrain from eating, and during the other twelve hours, you enjoy your meals. This fast is great for beginners because the fasting window is small and easy to accomplish. You can simply stop eating at 6:30 at night and begin eating at 6:30 in the morning. This prevents you from being hungry, but you are able to enjoy the benefits of a planned fast. The benefits will be further increased if you choose to exercise before you break your fast.

16/8

The 16/8 fast is similar to the 12/12 fast; only it has a longer fasting window. Also known as the Leangains diet, you fast for sixteen hours of the day and enjoy large meals during the remaining eight hours. If you try the 12/12 fast and don't experience the benefits you hope for, then you can try the 16/8 for more intense weight loss and health boosts.

Oftentimes due to the longer fasting window, men will choose to go the full sixteen hours, whereas some women will choose to go fourteen hours instead. When completing this fast, many people will finish their evening meal at eight in the evening and then simply skip breakfast the next morning before enjoying a large lunch at noon.

People often fall into this type of fasting naturally. While it may be different from what you are used to now, people naturally fall into eating habits. For instance, you are likely to feel hungry at the same time every day. That means that once you regularly practice the 16/8 fast, it will feel natural and easy. You simply will be unlikely to feel hungry during the fasting window.

One study of a 16/8 hour fast on mice was quite successful. In this study, it found that by limiting the eating window for mice to eight hours, they were able to decrease inflammation, reduce diabetes, treat liver disease, and greatly lose weight and treat obesity. These benefits were experienced even when the mice consumed as many calories as they wanted.

2 Days Every 5 Days

Fasting two days a week, also known as the 5:2 fast, is when a person eats the same amount of food, they otherwise would five days a week. On the other two days, instead of fully fasting without food, the person will consume a small number of calories. Women will usually eat five-hundred calories on fasting days, whereas men will consume six-hundred. These calories should be from healthy sources of protein and fats to help keep you satisfied. It's also important that you don't do both of your weekly fasts two days in a row. Give your body a chance to refuel between fasting days. This may mean that you fast on Tuesdays and Thursdays.

Weekly 24-Hour Fast

Some people choose to do a once-weekly twenty-four hour fast. Unlike the previously mentioned fast, people don't eat anything during this fast. However, it is easier than it sounds. This is because you don't start the fast until after either breakfast or lunch. You can fuel up in the morning to keep you going until the following afternoon. This makes the fast quite simple but extremely effective for weight loss and health benefits. However, it is still more difficult than the shorter fasts we have mentioned. If you are new to this, then I suggest starting with a 16/8 fast and slowly increasing the fasting window until it feels natural. Thankfully, this type of fast is much more natural when you are in the process of ketosis since your body will have ketones to sustain it.

When you aren't fasting, it's important to be sure that you eat your normal macro ratio in order to prevent any deficiencies or too little protein.

Chapter 7: Customizing Your Workout Routine

When people are trying to lose weight, they often restrict their calorie intake and increase their regular exercise. When this doesn't work, people will often further restrict calories and increase exercise even further. This may seem productive, but it is, in fact, counterproductive. Losing weight isn't as simple as expending more energy than we consume. While it may seem straightforward and reasonable, I'm sure you have experienced or seen other people experience the frustration this causes when it doesn't work. The problem is that by attempting to lose weight in this way, people's cortisol levels rise, and they become increasingly hungry. In the end, most people will end up both overeating and overexercising causing weight gain and increased inflammation.

Thankfully, you don't have to live this way. Not only is it ineffective, but there are many better ways to lose weight. The ketogenic diet has been shown to have incredible weight loss benefits, especially when paired with exercise. Not only does the ketogenic diet keep you full and satisfied for long periods, but it even boosts the benefits from your workout. One study found that when a person is on a low-carb diet, they are able to burn two to three times as much fat during exercise than people on high-carb diets. This is especially beneficial for people who are busy or disabled. Rather than having to expend a long time exercising to get little benefit, you can make the most out of a short workout.

The ketogenic diet can even boost your energy, making your workout routine easier. This is because people who are on a high-carb diet will often experience a drop in blood glucose during their workout. On the other hand, someone on the ketogenic diet is sustained by fats, protein, and ketones during their workout. These fuel sources are much more sustaining and long-lasting, making it perfect for a variety of people.

However, it's important not to begin a hardcore workout when you first begin the ketogenic diet. Remember, you may experience the keto flu, and you will have a difficult time performing a more physically intense exercise. Instead, allow yourself to adjust to the ketosis process for a few weeks and, in the meantime, focus on light to moderate exercises.

It's important to know that intense exercise that lasts longer than ten seconds, and less than two minutes is processed by the body differently than other exercises. These types require ATP energy and the glycogen that is usually stored in muscles. Examples of these are high-intensity interval training (HIIT) and bodybuilding. Since these two types of exercises require ATP energy, we often don't have enough glucose within our muscles on the ketogenic diet to do these as well as we otherwise would. For this reason, people who enjoy these workouts may want to follow the Targeted Ketogenic Diet or the Cyclical Ketogenic Diet. These two forms of the ketogenic diet are made specifically for people who prefer high-intensity workouts and athletes.

Although, people are able to excel on most exercises on the standard ketogenic diet. Endurance, moderate, and flexibility exercises don't require this ATP energy and are able to do quite well without carbs. For instance, aerobics are quite successful.

Cardio exercises such as cycling, running, rowing, stair-stepping, dancing, and sports are all great options on the ketogenic diet. In fact, they have more benefits than solely weight loss. Many people in today's modern society do not get the exercise they need. We sit at desks, in our cars, and on the couch. This only causes our health to degrade more quickly as we age and increases our risk of disease. But, studies have shown that the use of a moderate amount of cardio can strengthen our muscles, increase blood sugar control, improve lung health, increase memory, boost mental health, promote better sleep, increase blood flow to the brain, and more. There are quite a few reasons to add cardio to your schedule two or three times a week. Whether you hope to lose weight or increase your health, there are ample reasons to add cardio to your life.

When you are working out with cardio, it's important that you track your heart rate in order to receive the benefits. The recommendation is that your heart rate is between fifty and seventy percent of two-hundred and twenty, minus your age. This means that if you are thirty-years-old, then your target zone is between ninety-five and one-hundred and thirty-three. When you first start out, you can aim for the lower end of that zone, so about ninety-five. But, as you adjust to cardio and the ketogenic diet, then you can push yourself to get a higher heart rate and increased benefits.

One way you can begin is to simply perform an exercise for ten to fifteen minutes at the lowest end of your target range. You can do this a few times a week. Then, as you adjust, you simply add five minutes onto it every now and then until you work up to thirty to forty-five minutes. After you are adjusted to working out for longer periods, you can then work at increasing the intensity slightly in order to increase your heart rate.

Along with cardio exercises, flexibility exercises are ideal on the ketogenic diet. This includes yoga, pilates, and tai chi. These exercises are perfect for people who desire a more calming workout and who would like to increase their range of motion and decrease their risk of injury. Even if you prefer more intense exercises, such as cardio or bodybuilding, you can benefit from adding flexibility exercises to your routine. Some of the benefits include decreased stress, lower inflammation, improved muscle tone, improved posture, increased lung function, relaxed muscles, decreased strain on the joints, increased strength, and increased muscle control.

People used to regularly recommend that you stretch before you begin your workout. However, it has since been found that it's not very effective when used this way. Instead, you should warm-up with a more mild form of the workout you will be performing. For instance, if you play basketball, you could practice tossing some baskets. If you play volleyball, you may practice serving or receiving the ball. By doing this, you can warm up the exact muscles you will be using and decrease the chance of developing an injury. Do this for five to ten minutes, and you will be set.

This doesn't mean that stretches and flexibility exercises can't help people in sports, simply that doing them directly prior to the workout won't help. Instead, it is better to practice flexibility exercises on a daily basis to receive their benefits as well as using them to cool down after you finish a workout or routine.

These exercises often seem simple to people at first. They look at yoga and think it can't be too hard. But, there is much more to them than it may appear. You can't simply jump into these exercises and expect to excel. It takes practice to be able to fully complete them. For instance, if you begin bodybuilding and immediately want to lift a one-hundred-pound weight, you are only going to injure yourself. The same is true of flexibility exercises. Instead, start with a simple beginner level stretched and work your way up.

Take it slowly, and you will soon improve and receive many benefits throughout your daily life and within your other exercises or sports.

Chapter 8: Recipes

Just because you are no longer eating junk food and high carbohydrate dishes that set you up for a blood sugar crash doesn't mean you can't enjoy yourself. In this chapter, you will receive a wealth of recipes that will satisfy both your stomach and your taste buds. Get ready to discover some new mother watering favorites that you won't want to stop making. You will soon find dishes that you can enjoy on your own or wow the entire family with.

1. Ketorific Coffee

This coffee is the perfect addition to your morning. Not only will the caffeine help wake you up, but the medium-chain triglycerides from the coconut oil will increase ketone production and boost your energy throughout the day. It may seem weird to add butter to your coffee, but butter is simply cream. The reason you are using the butter is that it is grass-fed and contains many more health benefits. Not only that, but grass-fed butter tastes amazing and will make this rich coffee decadent.

But if you don't like coffee, don't worry. You can simply replace the coffee with tea or even add the ingredients to a low-carb shake.

Ketorific Coffee makes one serving, contains one-hundred and eighty-eight calories for each serving, and twenty-one grams of fat.

Ingredients:

- 8 oz. coffee, hot

- 1 tbsp. butter

- 1 tbsp. coconut or MCT oil

- ¼ tsp. vanilla

- A dash cinnamon (optional)

- Stevia® sweetener to taste (optional)

Instructions:

1. Using a blender, combine the hot coffee or tea with the remaining ingredients. Pour into a cup and enjoy!

2. Almond Flour Waffles

Who doesn't love waffles for breakfast? These are the perfect treat for a weekend family fun treat. But, what can you top waffles with when you can't use high-carb maple syrup? Firstly, there is a maple-flavored syrup option that is completely low-carb! Lanakto brand has a wonderful syrup that is sweetened with sugar alcohol. However, topping these waffles with berries, whipped cream, and Lily's® brand stevia-sweetened chocolate chips is divine.

Almond Flour Waffles makes six servings, contains two-hundred and thirty-six calories for each serving, ten grams of protein, nineteen grams of fat, and four net carbohydrates.

Ingredients:

- ¾ cup almond flour
- 2 tbsps. hemp hearts
- 2 tbsps. coconut flour
- 2 tsps. baking powder
- 1 ½ tsp. maple flavoring
- ¼ tsp. baking soda
- 1 tsp. Swerve® sweetener
- 5 eggs, separated
- ¼ cup half-and-half

- ¼ cup sour cream

- 2 tbsps. water

- 2 tbsps. butter, melted

Instructions:

1.   Allow the eggs to come to room temperature. However, if you don't have time to wait to let them sit out, there is a quick method. Simply place the eggs in hot water from the tap for five minutes. Afterward, separate the yolks from the whites.

2.   In a large clean bowl, place the egg whites and, using a hand mixer, whip them until they begin to form stiff peaks. In a separate bowl, combine the egg yolks, half and half, sour cream, water, maple flavoring, Swerve sweetener, almond flour, hemp hearts, and coconut flour.

3.   Add the melted butter, baking powder, and baking soda into the bowl of egg yolks and flour. Gently fold in the egg whites with a spatula just until combined and there are no white streaks remaining. However, be careful not to over mix the batter.

4.   Oil a preheated waffle iron and cook the waffle batter according to the individual iron's manufacture ring instructions. This usually takes about four minutes.

3. Egg-Stuffed Roasted Avocado

One of the best fat sources you can eat is avocados. This dish makes use of this heavenly fruit by stuffing it with eggs and then roasting it and topping it with melted cheese, crispy bacon, and freshly diced tomato. This dish is perfect for breakfast, lunch, or dinner.

Egg-Stuffed Roasted Avocados makes one serving, contains five-hundred and forty-seven calories, twenty-two grams of protein, forty-four grams of fat, and six net carbohydrates.

Ingredients:

- 1 avocado, medium

- 2 eggs

- 1 piece bacon, cooked and chopped

- 1 tbsp. cheddar cheese

- ½ tsp. sea salt

- ½ Roma tomato, diced

- A dash black pepper

Instructions:

1.   Begin by preheating the oven to 425°F and preparing a muffin pan for the avocado.

2.   Cut the avocado in half, remove the pit, scoop out a very small amount of the filling bigger. Place the avocados facing upward in the muffin tins so that the shape of the tin holds the avocado halves in place. Then, crack your eggs into the centers of the avocado halves.

3.   Sprinkle the top of the avocado with your salt, cheese, cooked chopped bacon, and diced tomato.

Allow it to cook in the oven until the egg is set, about fourteen to sixteen minutes.

4. Bacon Cheese Frittata with Kale

One of the best fat sources you can eat is avocados. This dish makes use of this heavenly fruit by stuffing it with eggs and then roasting it and topping it with melted cheese, crispy bacon, and freshly diced tomato. This dish is perfect for breakfast, lunch, or dinner.

Bacon Cheese Frittata with Kale makes five servings, contains two-hundred and forty-nine calories, sixteen grams of protein, eighteen grams of fat, and three net carbohydrates.

Ingredients:

- 10 eggs

- 3 cups kale, chopped

- A dash black pepper

- 1/3 cup cherry tomatoes, cut in half

- 4 slices bacon, cooked and chopped

- 4 oz. cheddar cheese, shredded

- ½ cup Half-and-half

- 1 tsp. sea salt

Instructions:

1.   While the oven is preheating to 350°F, begin to whisk together the eggs with the half and half. Add in the sea salt, black pepper, and bacon.

2.   In a large skillet over medium heat, cook down the kale until it is soft and wilted, about five minutes. Add in the eggs and top it off with the sliced cherry tomatoes and the cheddar cheese.

3.   Allow the frittata to continue cooking on the stove for five minutes and then place it in the oven to finish cooking for ten to twelve minutes. Once the eggs are fully cooked, remove them from the oven and serve.

5. Faux Mexican Cheesy Rice

The "rice" in this dish may actually be a low-carb vegetable, but that doesn't mean it is lacking in any of the flavors. This one-pan meal is quick and easy to prepare, making it perfect for a family meal or an indulgent cheesy dish for one.

Faux Mexican Cheesy Rice makes six servings, contains three-hundred and sixty-six calories for each serving, twenty-three grams of protein, twenty-five grams of fat, and seven net carbohydrates.

Ingredients:

- 1 pound ground beef, 85/15 fat

- ½ cup chicken or beef broth

- 12 oz. cauliflower rice

- 1 medium onion, diced

- ½ cup red bell pepper, diced

- 3 tbsps. taco seasoning

- ½ cup Roma tomatoes, diced

- 1 avocado

- 1 ½ cup cheddar cheese, shredded

- ¼ cup cilantro, chopped

Instructions:

1.   Over medium-high heat, place the ground 85/15 beef into a large skillet and allow it to brown until it's almost completely cooked through and hardly any pink is remaining. At this point, you want to add in the diced medium onion and the diced red bell pepper. Continue to cook the skillet until there is no pink remaining in the ground beef and stir in the taco seasoning.

2.   Stir in the cauliflower rice, either fresh or frozen, along with the diced Roma tomatoes and the chicken or beef broth. Allow the broth to simmer over medium-low heat to cook the cauliflower rice until it is softened. This process should take about eight to ten minutes of your cauliflower rice is frozen.

3.   Once the cauliflower is cooked, sprinkle the cheddar cheese over the top of the skillet, cover it with a lid, and allow it to cook for about three to four minutes until melted. Remove the skillet from the heat and top it with avocado, chopped cilantro, and any other favorite taco toppings.

6. <u>One Pan Creamy Garlic Chicken with Lemon</u>

There is no need to make the entire kitchen a mess for a nice dinner. Instead, you can enjoy these delicious seared chicken thighs in a creamy garlic sauce with shallots. Whether you want to impress someone for date night at home or to enjoy a luxurious yet simple meal by yourself, this dish is sure to please.

One Pan Creamy Garlic Chicken with Lemon makes four servings, contains four-hundred and sixty-nine calories for each serving, twenty-six grams of protein, thirty-seven grams of fat, and four net carbohydrates.

Ingredients:

- 4 chicken thighs (boneless and skinless)

- 1 cup chicken broth

- ¼ cup heavy cream

- 2 tbsps. lemon juice

- 1 tbsp. olive oil

- 2 tbsps. butter

- A dash black pepper, ground

- 4 garlic cloves, minced

- ¼ cup shallot, minced

- ½ tsp. red pepper flakes

- 2 tbsps. basil, chopped

- 1 tsp. sea salt

Instructions:

1.   Place the boneless and skinless chicken thighs between two sheets of plastic wrap and pound them with a mallet until they are about half an inch in even thickness. Peel off the plastic and sprinkle both sides of the chicken thighs with sea salt and black pepper.

2.   Preheat the oven to a temperature of 375°F and while it is warming up, sear the chicken. To do this, place the chicken thighs in a large skillet with olive oil over medium-high heat. It should take about two to three minutes in order to sear both sides. You aren't trying to cook the chicken all the way through, as you will finish it off in the oven. Once the chicken is done searing, place it on a plate.

3.   Pour the chicken broth, red pepper flakes, shallots, lemon juice, and garlic into the skillet that you have removed the chicken from. Whisk it around so that any pieces of chicken that might be stuck to the pan dislodge and cook in the broth. Bring the heat up to medium-high and allow the chicken broth shallot mixture to simmer for ten to fifteen minutes. You want

to allow the sauce to condense until there is only about one-third of a cup remaining.

4.   After the chicken garlic sauce has condensed, whisk in the butter, allowing it to melt. Remove the skillet from the heat and whisk in the heavy cream before placing it back on the heat for an additional thirty seconds without allowing the cream sauce to boil.

5.   Place the chicken in the skillet and allow it to roast in the sauce in the preheated oven until fully cooked and reaching an internal temperature of one-hundred and sixty-five degrees, about five to eight minutes. Remove the chicken from the oven and top it with chopped basil.

7. Cheeseburger Pie

This cheeseburger pie is a family favorite. It's perfect when made exactly to the recipe, but you can also top it with your favorite burger ingredients. Not only that, but this pie is easy to prepare for a crowd and full of nutrient-rich protein.

Cheeseburger Pie makes eight servings, contains two-hundred and eighty calories for each serving, seventeen grams of protein, twenty-one grams of fat, and three net carbohydrates.

Ingredients:

- 1 pund ground 80/20 beef
- 4 eggs
- 1 cup almond milk
- 1/3 cup coconut flour
- 3 tbsps. almond flour
- 1 cup onion, diced
- 1 ½ cheddar cheese
- 1 tsp. sea salt
- 1 tsp. baking powder
- 1 Roma tomato, diced
- 1 tsp. Worcestershire sauce

Instructions:

1.   Place the ground beef and the Worcestershire sauce in a large skillet and allow it to cook over medium-high heat until it is browned, about eight to ten minutes. Stir the sea salt into the ground beef.

2.   In a bowl, combine the eggs, almond flour, coconut flour, almond milk, and baking powder, and then pour it into the skillet over the cooked ground beef. Add the cheese and onions to the top of the skillet dish and bake the cheeseburger pie in a preheated oven at 400°F. Remove the cheeseburger pie from the oven after twenty-five minutes.

3.   Top the pie with tomatoes, slice, and enjoy.

8. Shrimp and Sausage Skillet

This shrimp and sausage skillet is incredibly easy and quick. It only requires one pan, and all you have to do is add all of the ingredients together, and within ten minutes, you have a tasty meal. When picking out your sausage, try to find one that is healthy with few ingredients and higher in fat.

Shrimp and Sausage Skillet makes six servings, contains three-hundred and fifty-three calories for each serving, fifteen grams of protein, twenty-six grams of fat, and ten net carbohydrates.

Ingredients:

- 1 pound shrimp, deveined and peeled

- 14 oz. healthy pork sausage, sliced

- 2 tbsps. olive oil

- 2 tsps. cajun seasoning

- 1 bell pepper, diced

- 1 pound asparagus, sliced into bite-sized pieces

- 2 medium zuccchini, sliced

- ½ cup onion, diced

Instructions:

1.   In a large skillet, cook the sausage, shrimp, vegetables, and seasonings together over medium-high heat in the olive oil until it is fully cooked and the shrimp is pink about seven to eight minutes.

9. Bacon Cauliflower Gratin

With this delicious gratin, you won't miss potatoes at all. The sauce is made with decadent cream, butter, cheese, and bacon. Whether you want to make this at the beginning of the week to enjoy with a variety of meals or as a dish to serve at family dinner, this gratin is sure to please. While you can certainly use fresh cauliflower for this dish, it is made simple and easy if you choose to use frozen florets instead.

Bacon Cauliflower Gratin makes six servings, contains two-hundred and fifty-five calories for each serving, eight grams of protein, twenty-two grams of fat, and four net carbohydrates.

Ingredients:

- 1 pound cauliflower florets

- 1 cup almond milk

- ½ cup heavy cream

- 2 tbsps. butter

- 4 tsps. coconut flour

- 4 tsps. almond flour

- ¾ tsp. sea salt

- 1 cup cheddar cheese, grated

- ¼ tsp. onion powder

- 4 bacon strips, chopped

- ¼ tsp. garlic powder

- A dash black pepper

Instructions:

1. Place the cauliflower florets in a pot of boiling water while the oven preheats to 375°F. While the cauliflower boils, cook the bacon in a skillet until crispy.

2. Once the bacon is cooked, remove it from the pan, add in the butter and allow it to melt into the bacon fat. Once fully melted, whisk in your coconut flour and almond flour and allow it to brown and create a nutty aroma, about one minute. Watch the flour carefully and continue to whisk it, as it can burn quickly.

3. Add heavy cream, almond milk, garlic powder, sea salt, onion powder, and pepper into the almond flour mixture and whisk them until it is smooth without lumps. Bring it to a boil and then letter simmer over medium heat until it is quite thick, about eight minutes. Remove the mixture from the heat and stir in the bacon and half of the shredded cheddar cheese until melted and combined.

4. Once the cauliflower is tender, after about five to seven minutes, drain the water and press the

cauliflower florets between two towels in order to dry them as much as possible.

5.   In a small eight by eight-inch square baking dish, spread a third of the bacon cheese sauce and top it with the cauliflower. Over the cauliflower, pour the remainder of the cheese sauce and then sprinkle the top of the dish with the remaining half of the shredded cheese.

6.   Bake the bacon cauliflower gratin in the oven until the top is golden and bubbly, about twenty-five to thirty minutes. If you want to make the top extra crispy, you can turn the oven's broiler on for the last two to three minutes.

10. Parmesan Sun-Dried Tomato Zucchini

This dish is perfect when you want to enjoy an Italian flare. The Parmesan and sun-dried tomatoes pair perfectly with the mild zucchini and the salty, crispy bacon.

Parmesan Sun-Dried Tomato Zucchini makes four servings, contains one-hundred and eighty-eight calories for each serving, nine grams of protein, thirteen grams of fat, and six net carbohydrates.

Ingredients:

- 3 zucchini, sliced into half-inch pieces

- 1/3 cup sun-dried tomatoes, chopped

- ½ cup parmesan, shredded

- 4 slices bacon slices, chopped

- 1/3 cup onion, sliced

- ¾ tsp. sea salt

Instructions:

1.   In a large skillet, cook the chopped bacon slices over medium-high heat until they become crispy. Remove the bacon from the pan for use later on.

2.   After the bacon is removed from the pan, reduce the heat to medium and add in the sliced zucchini pieces and sliced onion to cook in the bacon fat until just beginning to soften. The zucchini should require between five and seven minutes to reach this stage. Add in the chopped sun-dried tomatoes and allow it to cook together until the zucchini is softened, about an extra five minutes.

3.   Stir the cooked bacon and the shredded Parmesan into the zucchini dish and season with sea salt. Taste the zucchini and adjust the seasonings to your preferences.

11. Garlic Butter Mushrooms

These decadent mushrooms are perfect for an appetizer or side dish, especially when served with steak, shrimp, or low-carb "pasta" options. These mushrooms are not only low-carb; they are also full of vital nutrients, making them a great addition to your daily diet.

Garlic Butter Mushrooms makes four servings, contains one-hundred and seventy-eight calories for each serving, three grams of protein, fifteen grams of fat, and six net carbohydrates.

Ingredients:

- 1 pound button or crimini mushrooms

- ¼ cup butter

- 1 tbsp. olive oil

- 2 tbsps. chicken stock

- 2 tbsps. parsley, chopped

- 1 tsp. thyme, chopped

- 4 garlic cloves, large, minced

- Sea salt and black pepper

Instructions:

1. Melt the butter (ideally grass-fed) in a large skillet and cook the mushrooms over medium-high heat until

they turn golden and begin to crisp around the edges, about five minutes.

2.   Pour in the chicken stock and allow it to reduce for two minutes before adding in the garlic, thyme, and parsley. Cook for an additional minute until the herbs and garlic are fragrant. Add sea salt and black pepper to your individual taste. Garnish with extra parsley, if desired.

12. Vegetable Antipasto Salad

This antipasto salad is a wonderful way to get your protein and fat fix without much work. You can simply make a large batch of this salad at the beginning of the week and enjoy it for lunch. This salad is dense in nutrients and calories, so when it is served with six servings, it is a full meal. However, if you eat it in smaller servings, it could be a wonderful side dish.

Vegetable Antipasto Salad makes six servings, contains four-hundred and twenty-eight calories for each serving, twenty grams of protein, thirty-four grams of fat, and six net carbohydrates.

Ingredients:

- 12 oz. cauliflower florets, chopped

- 4 oz. hard salami, chopped

- 4 oz. hard pepperoni, chopped

- 4 oz. provolone cheese, chopped

- 4 oz. mozzarella, preferably fresh

- 1 cup cherry tomatoes, sliced in half

- 1 English cucumber, sliced

- 1 cup roasted red peppers, chopped

- 1/3 cup olive oil

- 2 tbsps. Dijon mustard

- 1/3 cup apple cider vinegar

- 1 tbsp. Italian seasoning

- 3 garlic cloves, minced

- 2 tsps. Swerve® sweetener

- Sea salt and pepper

Instructions:

1. In a medium-sized bowl, vigorously whisk together the olive oil, apple cider vinegar, Dijon mustard, Italian seasoning, sweetener, garlic, sea salt, and black pepper until they are well combined. Taste and adjust the salt to your preference.

2. In a large bowl, toss together the vegetables, cheeses, and meats with the freshly made vinaigrette.

3. Place the antipasto salad in the fridge and allow the ingredients to marinate together for a minimum of two hours before serving. You can even make this salad a couple of days ahead of eating it.

13. Mashed Cauliflower with Horseradish and Garlic

Mashed Cauliflower with Horseradish and Garlic makes eight servings, contains one-hundred and twenty-four calories for each serving, four grams of protein, nine grams of fat, and five net carbohydrates.

Ingredients:

- 1 head or 2 pounds cauliflower florets

- 1 ½ tbsp. prepared horseradish

- 4 garlic cloves, minced

- 3 tbsps. butter

- ½ cup parmesan cheese, grated

- ½ cup sour cream

- 5 chives, chopped

- Sea salt and black pepper

Instructions:

1. Steam the cauliflower in either the microwave or on the stove until tender. If you are steaming it on the stove, you can expect it to take about fifteen minutes. Drain the water from the cauliflower and pat it dry with a towel to remove excess liquid

2. After the cauliflower is dry, mash it with a potato masher or an immersion blender. Add in the butter,

horseradish, minced garlic, sour cream, Parmesan cheese, and seasonings. Continue to mash until all of the ingredients are fully combined.

3.   Once the cauliflower mash is your preferred consistency, top it off with the chopped chives.

14. Peanut Butter Fudge Fat Bombs

Fat bombs can be a wonderful addition to the ketogenic diet, especially during the beginning. The longer you are in ketosis, the less hungry you will be. Yet, when you first begin the process of ketosis, you might find that you get hungry and weak more frequently. But, if you enjoy a fat bomb when you are feeling this way, you can experience a great increase in energy and satisfaction. This particular fat bomb is inspired by peanut butter fudge and is sure to please any peanut lover.

This antipasto salad is a wonderful way to get your protein and fat fix without much work. You can simply make a large batch of this salad at the beginning of the week and enjoy it for lunch. This salad is dense in nutrients and calories, so when it is served with six servings, it is a full meal. However, if you eat it in smaller servings, it could be a wonderful side dish.

Peanut Butter Fudge Fat Bomb makes eight servings, contains two-hundred and eight calories for each serving, three grams of protein, twenty grams of fat, and three net carbohydrates.

Ingredients:

- ½ cup natural sugar-free peanut butter
- ¼ cup grass-fed butter
- MCT oil - .25 oil

- 3 tbsps. Swerve® confectioner sweetener
- ¼ tsp. vanilla
- A dash sea salt

The Instructions:

1. In a small bowl whip, together all of the peanut butter fat bomb ingredients with a hand mixer.

2. Divide the mixture between eight silicone candy molds and let it set up in the fridge until they can be easily removed, about thirty minutes. Store the fat bombs in the fridge or freezer.

15. Keto Chocolate

This simple to make chocolate is delicious and perfectly keto-friendly! Better yet, it is highly customizable. You can easily add your favorite ingredients such as nut butter, chopped nuts, berries, chia seeds, and more.

Keto Chocolate makes ten servings, contains one-hundred and fifty-five calories for each serving, one gram of protein, seventeen grams of fat, and two net carbohydrates.

Ingredients:

- ¾ cup cocoa powder

- ¾ cup coconut oil

- 1 tsp. vanilla extract

- A dash sea salt

- Swerve® confectioner sweetener to taste

Instructions:

1.   Over medium-low heat, melt the coconut oil and add in the cocoa powder and Swerve confectioner sweetener. Remove from heat and add in the sea salt and vanilla extract.

2.   Divide the keto chocolate between twenty silicone candy molds and allow them to freeze until hardened, about twenty minutes.

3.   Store the chocolate in the fridge at all times. Two pieces are one serving.